C000150986

B-199675

To the President of the Senate and the
Speaker of the House of Representatives

    This report discusses the Air Force's logistics support
planning for the F-16 aircraft and how substantial reductions
in support costs can be achieved. It also suggests logistics
alternatives which, we believe, can improve F-16 logistics
support planning.

    We initiated this review after preliminary research indi-
cated that problems existed in the Air Force's planning for
the integrated logistics support program for the F-16 aircraft. This review is an important aspect of our continuing
efforts to recommend logistics management improvements in the
Department of Defense.

    We are sending copies of this report to the Director,
Office of Management and Budget; the Secretary of Defense;
and the Secretary of the Air Force.

Comptroller General
of the United States

F-16 INTEGRATED LOGISTICS
SUPPORT: STILL TIME TO
CONSIDER ECONOMICAL
ALTERNATIVES

D I G E S T

This report evaluates the F-16 aircraft's
integrated logistics support plan, identi-
fies the status of several of the plan's
logistics elements, and concludes that
while the plan should ensure that aircraft
will be adequately maintained, support costs
can be reduced and the aircraft's effectiveness can be improved.

The F-16 is being developed in a cooperative
undertaking between the United States and
four European North Atlantic Treaty Organization countries. The current program provides for coproduction of 1,113 aircraft--
348 for the four European countries, 650
for the United States, 75 for Israel, and
40 for Egypt.

An integrated logistics support plan was
developed to coordinate and control the logistics tasks necessary to support the aircraft but the plan has had little influence
on subsystem selections and support because

--the F-16 was a prototype program and integrated logistics support was not included in the prototype contract and

--the first integrated logistics support
   plan was not final until 10 months after
   the aircraft entered full-scale development.

The plan includes logistics support analysis, a process set up to collect and retain
information on equipment, maintenance,
repair parts, and critical F-16 components.
Since the single data base required for logistics support analysis has not been developed, updating changes to logistics support data will be difficult. Once developed, however, it should benefit the F-16
during its remaining life cycle.

Tear Sheet. Upon removal, the report
cover date should be noted hereon.

i

LCD-80-89

GAO and others have identified alternative operational and support procedures which, if implemented, could greatly reduce F-16 support costs.

The Air Force could save $56 million in avionics equipment by centralizing intermediate maintenance in Europe and the United States. Centralization would also reduce requirements for personnel, equipment, and facilities. Although several agencies have recommended centralization, the Air Force continues to plan for decentralized support because it is concerned about the vulnerability/survivability of a centralized facility. However, the Air Force is studying the feasibility of centralization.

A Memorandum of Understanding with the European participating governments commits the United States to having Europeans do depot repair for the F-16 aircraft in Europe. However, the Air Force is moving slowly toward obtaining this European support. Unless the Air Force accelerates negotiations, only limited support will be available when the U.S. F-16s activate in Europe. If the Air Force does not use European participating governments' depot repair, industrial participation terms of the Memorandum of Understanding may not be met.

Traditionally, the Air Force provides a 10-percent backup aircraft inventory for depot maintenance and modification. However, GAO questions the need for this number of backup aircraft because the F-16 was designed to eliminate planned depot maintenance and overhaul. The actual number of backup aircraft needed for the F-16 program is not known, but the Air Force is planning to buy 110. Reducing the inventory could save up to $1.4 billion.

Although the Air Force researched the benefits of simulation over conventional hardware before deciding to buy the simulated aircraft maintenance trainer, it did not adequately consider training alternatives in the event the delivery of the simulator was delayed. Because it underestimated the time needed to develop the trainer, the Air Force now has to change the maintenance training program to work around the trainer's limited capabilities. The operational uncertainties of the maintenance trainers need to be resolved promptly and contingency plans provided in case of further delivery delays.

Portions of the F-16's pilot training equipment--the weapon system trainer--are still being developed, and as a result, Air Force planners do not know exactly how often these trainers will be used. Since the Air Force already has decided to install a complete weapon system trainer at each F-16 base, at a unit cost of $65 million, it could be buying more training equipment than needed. Centralizing training units or using different trainer components which can provide independent training at some locations are worthwhile options the Air Force should consider.

The Air Force must have fully tested technical orders, which explain how to install, operate, and repair aircraft and related equipment, before it can do maintenance work. However, many F-16 technical orders were not usable. Since many of the complex orders are still to be developed, the Air Force, by providing sufficient resources to the technical order validation/verification process and requiring more frequent comprehensive inspections of the orders, has an excellent opportunity to improve order quality.

The F-16 integrated logistics support plan does not include the time needed to design and fabricate mobile shelters which may be needed to deploy the expensive avionics test equipment. Also, the plan has not been updated to show the new leadtimes needed to build facilities at bases receiving the F-16. An updated integrated logistics support plan and accelerated completion of shelters for avionics equipment are needed.

RECOMMENDATIONS

The Air Force should act upon the operational and logistics support procedures

discussed in this report before deploying the
F-16. GAO recommends that the Secretary
of Defense direct the Air Force to

--centralize F-16 intermediate maintenance
  (p. 22),

--accelerate negotiations with the European
  participating countries for depot repair
  of U.S. F-16s in Europe (p. 23),

--reexamine the need for backup aircraft
  inventory (p. 23), and

--assess the cost/benefit of buying a weapon
  system trainer for every F-16 base (p. 29).

Other specific recommendations appear on
pages 23, 28, 33, 39, and 43.

AGENCY COMMENTS

The Department of Defense (DOD) commented
that the Air Force had identified several of
the areas discussed as requiring management
attention. DOD took exception to three
recommendations--centralizing maintenance,
eliminating or reducing backup aircraft inventory, and assessing the cost/benefit of
buying a weapon system trainer for every
F-16 base--but GAO found DOD's arguments
unconvincing.

Although generally disagreeing with the centralized maintenance concept, DOD said that
to assure the current logistics structure is
still valid, the Air Force is reexamining
centralization for F-16 intermediate maintenance. DOD's argument against reducing the
F-16 backup aircraft inventory is that the
10-percent inventory factor historically has
been accurate for tactical fighter aircraft.
However, because depot overhaul contributes
to the need for backup inventory and the F-16
is designed to reduce depot overhaul, GAO
believes the 10-percent factor for backup
aircraft should be reexamined.

DOD said that buying fewer weapon system
trainers was contrary to the Air Force's
position to collocate trainers with

operational and training units whenever
possible. Also, on the basis of DOD's
projected aircrew usage, one trainer is required for each location. Considering the
proximity of some bases and the unproven
usage data and high unit cost of weapon
system trainers, GAO believes the Air Force's
position on trainer collocation should be
reevaluated.

Contents

ABBREVIATIONS

DOD	Department of Defense
EPGs	European participating governments
GAO	General Accounting Office
ILS	integrated logistics support
LSA	logistics support analysis
NATO	North Atlantic Treaty Organization
SAMT	simulated aircraft maintenance trainer

CHAPTER 1

INTRODUCTION

The multibillion dollar F-16 aircraft program is a cooperative undertaking between the United States and four European North Atlantic Treaty Organization (NATO) countries. These four European participating governments (EPGs)--Belgium, Denmark, the Netherlands, and Norway--will coproduce the aircraft with the United States, an arrangement that should help standardize weapon systems in NATO, provide a low-cost fighter aircraft, and increase industrial activity for participants. The current program provides for coproduction of 1,113 F-16 aircraft--348 for EPGs, 650 for the United States, 75 for Israel, and 40 for Egypt.

The Memorandum of Understanding between the United States and the four EPGs is the basic charter for carrying out the F-16 multinational program. It commits the United States Government to place contracts with European industry equal to 58 percent of the procurement value of the 348 European aircraft. This will be accomplished by having the Europeans participate in the production of their own aircraft and the 650 U.S. aircraft. The Europeans will also participate in production of third country aircraft and perform depot repair on U.S. F-16s in Europe. The Air Force ultimately plans to buy 738 additional aircraft; however, EPG industry participation beyond the initial 650 Air Force program has not been determined.

The F-16 is a follow-on to the lightweight fighter prototype program which investigated the feasibility and usefulness of a highly maneuverable, low-cost fighter. The lightweight fighter was approved for prototyping in January 1972. The contractors, General Dynamics Corporation and the Northrup Corporation, each built and flew prototypes.

During late 1974, the Air Force evaluated the lightweight fighter prototypes and solicited full-scale development proposals from the contractors. In January 1975 the Air Force selected a derivative of the General Dynamics prototype, called the F-16, and awarded a full-scale development contract to General Dynamics shortly thereafter.

In December 1979 the Air Force estimated the procurement cost of each F-16 at $12.6 million and the total F-16 program cost at more than $18 billion.

SCOPE OF REVIEW

Our review of the Air Force's logistics support planning for the F-16 aircraft was initiated in response to broad congressional interest in reducing life cycle costs of major weapon systems.

We coordinated our audit work with the Air Force Audit Agency, which also is reviewing logistics support of the F-16. As agreed with the Air Force Audit Agency, we did not review the F-16's supply support program as it relates to the airframe of U.S. F-16s, since the Agency is doing an extensive audit of that area. The Agency's audit report is scheduled for publication in September 1980.

The information in this report is based on interviews with Air Force, contractor, and EPG officials; reviews of records, regulations, and reports provided by those officials; and research of published studies and reports. We made our review at:

--Headquarters, U.S. Air Force, the Pentagon.

--F-16 System Program Office and the Air Force Logistics Command, Wright-Patterson Air Force Base, Ohio.

--Tactical Air Command, Langley Air Force Base, Virginia.

--Air Training Command, Randolph Air Force Base, Texas.

--Ogden Air Logistics Center, Hill Air Force Base, Utah.

--General Dynamics Corporation, Forth Worth, Texas.

F-16 AIRCRAFT   SOURCE: GENERAL DYNAMICS

CHAPTER 2

INTEGRATED LOGISTICS SUPPORT PLANNING

FOR THE F-16 AIRCRAFT

The Air Force's logistics support planning should provide adequate support for the F-16 aircraft. However, like any new weapon system there are still unknowns which could affect the system's readiness and logistics support costs. The Air Force should consider alternative operational and support concepts to reduce the growing F-16 ownership costs.

INTEGRATED LOGISTICS SUPPORT
PLANNING IS NECESSARY

Effective logistics support planning for a new weapon system has become crucial since ownership costs of a system over its service life often exceed development and procurement costs. The integrated logistics support (ILS) concept is an attempt to lower ownership costs by creating an efficient logistics support system and by considering alternative requirements early enough in the acquisition cycle to change weapon system design or logistics support plans, if needed, while meeting program requirements.

Although the ILS concept can be implemented any time, new Department of Defense (DOD) guidance requires it at the very start of a weapon program to achieve the greatest results. As a program progresses, critical decisions must be made, and with each such decision, there remains less opportunity for ILS to influence the final product. Many critical decisions already have been made for the F-16 program, but the ILS plan can still be used to cut costs and to help planners in areas where decisions have not been completed.

Logistics support includes many tasks that affect many organizations. The principal elements of an ILS plan are (1) maintenance, (2) support and test equipment, (3) supply support, (4) packaging, handling, storage, and transportation, (5) technical data, (6) facilities, (7) personnel, (8) training and training devices, and (9) computer resources support.

ILS ensures that these support elements are integrated with other system requirements. Although each element is usually managed separately, all the other elements must be considered when planning, coordinating, and controlling all logistics support tasks necessary to support the major system.

ILS PROVIDES THE VEHICLE TO INTEGRATE SUPPORT
CONSIDERATIONS INTO WEAPON SYSTEM DESIGN

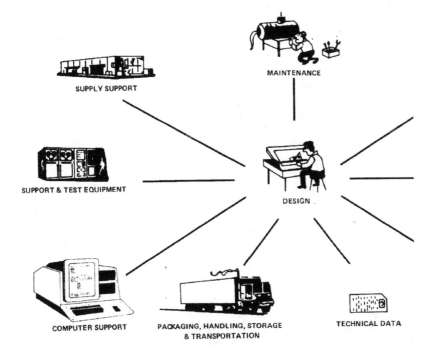

SUPPLY SUPPORT

MAINTENANCE

SUPPORT & TEST EQUIPMENT

DESIGN

COMPUTER SUPPORT

PACKAGING, HANDLING, STORAGE
& TRANSPORTATION

TECHNICAL DATA

An important tool of an effective ILS plan is logistics support analysis (LSA). LSA provides and maintains information on the performance of all logistics elements and emphasizes their interrelationships throughout the system design and development. DOD principles for LSA management state that the essentials of an LSA program are to

--analyze and define logistics support requirements,

--predict logistics support costs, and

--evaluate logistics alternatives.

LSA, the integrative force in the ILS plan, enables the ILS manager to evaluate and make decisions on the program as the aircraft design matures.

THE F-16 ILS PLAN IS LIMITED

The F-16 ILS plan was designed to coordinate and control the logistics tasks necessary to support the U.S. and EPG F-16s. Although the plan should provide adequate support for the first F-16 wing that reaches initial operating capability in 1981, it has had very little influence on the F-16's subsystem selections and support because:

--The F-16 was a prototype program and the ILS concept was not included in the prototype contract. Therefore, very little conceptual data was available as the aircraft entered full-scale development.

--The first ILS plan for the F-16 was not final until November 1975--10 months after the aircraft entered full-scale development.

The F-16's ILS plan includes an LSA process which collects and retains information on equipment, maintenance tasks, repair parts, and critical F-16 components. Although the DOD standard for LSA (Mil. Std. 1388-1) provides that early LSA efforts are of special importance in the acquisition cycle so it can influence the design of a weapon system and provide system supportability, the F-16 LSA process did not do this, because the ILS process did not begin until full-scale development.

LSA documentation is provided through an LSA record, a tool that the ILS manager uses during design for managing and acquiring the logistical support for the end item. For the LSA process to be effective, a single LSA record or data base should be developed. Although the Air Force used analytical techniques, such as Design to Cost, Life Cycle Cost, and

6

Optimum Repair Level Analysis, during the F-16's full-scale development, LSA was not fully implemented because of numerous errors in its data base and a lack of integrated data. Therefore, it will be difficult to update the changes to logistics support data resulting from tests, configuration changes, and operational use.

Although not available during full-scale development, as required by DOD directive, the LSA data base, once developed, should benefit the F-16 during its remaining life cycle by documenting

--the number and types of people required to support the aircraft,

--the instructions to conduct maintenance,

--the number and types of repair parts,

--the location of those repair parts, and

--test equipment and tools required.

F-16 LOGISTICS SUPPORT AREAS
NEEDING AIR FORCE ATTENTION

DOD has established criteria that should provide effective and affordable logistics support systems. The ILS directives and LSA standards provide a good guide to military logistics planners. Furthermore, compliance with these criteria can optimize the Nation's investment in defense capabilities.

The F-16 will play an important role in national defense. Because the F-16 program is still developing (see chart on p. 9), DOD and Air Force logistics planners will be making many more decisions to ensure that the F-16 program is successful. If they address the following problems and alternative procedures, their framework for a comprehensive approach to logistics support planning should improve.

--Centralizing intermediate maintenance in Europe and the United States. This could save the Air Force $56 million in avionics equipment. Centralization would also reduce requirements for personnel, equipment, and facilities. Although several agencies have recommended centralization, the Air Force continues to plan for decentralized support because it is concerned about the vulnerability/survivability of a centralized facility. However, it is studying the feasibility of centralization.

--Accelerating negotiations with EPGs to ensure depot
repair capability when U.S. F-16s arrive in Europe.
Although a Memorandum of Understanding with the
EPGs commits the United States to let Europeans do
depot repair for U.S. F-16 aircraft in Europe, the
Air Force is moving slowly toward obtaining the depot
support. As a result, only limited support will be
available when the U.S. F-16s activate in Europe. If
the Air Force does not use the EPGs' depot repair, the
industrial participation terms of the Memorandum
of Understanding may not be met.

--Reducing backup aircraft inventory. Traditionally,
the Air Force provides a 10-percent backup aircraft
inventory for depot maintenance and modification.
However, we question the need for this amount of backup
aircraft because the F-16 was designed to eliminate
planned depot maintenance and overhaul. The actual
number of backup aircraft needed for the F-16 program
is not known, but the Air Force is planning to buy
110 aircraft at a cost of $1.4 billion. While some
aircraft may be needed for the modification program,
these should only be funded after key decisions have
been made. Factors to be considered should include
(1) length of time needed to "button up" aircraft
and get them back to the units during emergencies
and (2) deployment schedules of units.

--Resolving the operational uncertainties of the simulated aircraft maintenance trainers and providing contingency plans in case delivery of trainers is delayed
further. Although the Air Force researched the benefits of simulation over conventional hardware before
deciding to buy the trainers, it did not adequately
consider training alternatives in the event of delay
in simulator delivery. Because the Air Force underestimated the time needed to develop this trainer,
it now finds the maintenance training program has to
be changed to work around the trainer's limited capabilities.

--Assessing the cost/benefit of buying a weapon system
trainer for every F-16 base. Portions of the F-16
pilot training equipment are still being developed,
and, as a result, Air Force planners do not know
exactly how often these trainers will be used.
Since the Air Force already has decided to install a
complete weapon system trainer at each F-16 base, at
a unit cost of $65 million, it could be buying more
training equipment than needed.

8

	1978	1979	1980	1981	1982	1983
Aircraft arrivals at Hill AFB						
First delivery	○	●				
Final delivery				●○		
Technical orders completed						
Organizational level		●	○			
Intermediate level (AIS)			●	○		
Depot level				●	○	
Air Force maintenance responsibility						
Organizational level		●	○			
Intermediate level			●○			
Depot level				●		○
Training program starts						
Pilot	●○					
Maintenance	● ○					
Training Equipment Deliveries						
Operational flight trainer			●	○		
Simulated Aircraft		□○				
Maintenance Trainer						

● Planned (original)
○ Actual or anticipated
□ Partial Delivery

9

--Providing sufficient resources to the technical order
   validation/verification process and requiring more frequent comprehensive inspections of technical orders.
   Technical orders, which describe maintenance procedures and must be available before Air Force personnel
   can work on equipment, should be delivered before or
   concurrently with the delivery of equipment. The management, development, and testing processes of the
   orders, however, show that this is not the case. The
   result has been poor quality orders with time consuming
   changes, forcing the Air Force to buy unplanned contractor maintenance support.

--Updating the ILS plan and accelerating completion of
   mobile shelters which are used to deploy the expensive
   avionics test equipment. The F-16 plan does not include the time needed to design and fabricate these
   shelters. Also, the plan has not been updated to show
   new leadtimes needed to build facilities at bases receiving the F-16.

CONCLUSION

The logistics support planned for the F-16 should provide
adequate support. However, the concerns discussed in this report point out a need for the Air Force to review the F-16
logistics support planning and to take advantage of opportunities to provide more effective and efficient support.

CHAPTER 3

F-16 MAINTENANCE PLANNING CAN BE IMPROVED

Generally, maintenance planning for the F-16 has been adequate. However, the Air Force may be able to reduce support costs and improve readiness. Maintenance costs are rising, and the Air Force annually spends hundreds of millions of dollars for weapon system maintenance alone. The Air Force can save some of these millions and at the same time improve its readiness by adopting alternative maintenance plans, such as

--centralizing intermediate maintenance for the F-16 in Europe and the United States,

--using the European participating countries' depot-level maintenance and overhaul facilities in Europe, and

--reducing its backup aircraft inventory.

CENTRALIZING INTERMEDIATE
MAINTENANCE WILL REDUCE COSTS

Centralizing intermediate maintenance in Europe and the United States will benefit the Air Force. Several agencies that recommend centralized intermediate maintenance for F-16s have acknowledged this. Yet, the Air Force continues to plan for decentralized support.

Since 1958 we and DOD have encouraged centralization to eliminate duplication and to improve effectiveness, efficiency, and economy. In July 1978 the House Committee on Appropriations recommended that the Air Force use this concept for future deployment of the F-16. Our March 1979 report 1/ pointed out that centralized support for the F-15 and F-16 aircraft could reduce the support resources needed. In response, the Deputy Assistant Secretary of the Air Force (Logistics) reported that the Air Force recognized the potential for savings available from centralizing aircraft component repair and was planning to examine the recommendations made. This examination should be completed in December 1980.

1/"Centralizing Air Force Aircraft Component Repair in the Field Can Provide Significant Savings" (LCD-79-409, Mar. 28, 1979).

Although the Air Force adopted a centralized intermediate repair concept for the F-4 and the A-10 aircraft, it has no current plans to do so for the F-16 in Europe and the United States. Air Force officials are concerned that centralizing F-16 facilities would prohibitively increase transportation and spare parts costs. They are also concerned with the vulnerability/survivability of the centralized facilities.

Intermediate maintenance as now planned for the United States and Europe will be done at each F-16 operating base. The maintenance team will be located with the unit and deployed with it in case of war. Although Air Force officials believe centralization will significantly increase spare parts and transportation costs, we believe these costs can be reduced and additional costs, if any, will be more than offset by the savings centralization will produce.

Spare parts

A primary Air Force concern is that centralization will be prohibitively expensive because as pipeline times (time the part is in the repair cycle, including packaging, transportation, and repair times) increase the number of spares required also increases. Air Force officials estimate that each additional day the spares pipeline time increases, costs rise by $1 million for each aircraft wing centrally supported.

However, we believe the cost of any additional spare parts requirements should be reduced, if not completely offset, because of the following:

--The Pacific Air Force F-4 experience with centralized maintenance demonstrated that the quality of repair improved. This should reduce repair times, decrease failure rates, and reduce the number of spares needed.

--The Pacific Air Force also found that items that had previously been sent to depot for repair could be repaired at the intermediate level. As a result, spares requirements should decrease since intermediate level pipeline time is only 10 days compared to 60 days for depot level.

--Since more testing and repair equipment would be available, time to repair equipment would decrease. For example, a centralized repair facility with three avionics test sets would have at least one test set available 97 percent of the time, while a unit with one test set would have repair capability only 70 percent of the time. Therefore, a reduction in waiting time means reduced pipeline times, saving spares dollars.

Transportation

Air Force officials feel that transportation costs for a centralized facility would increase significantly. But, experience in the Pacific has shown that transportation costs can be reduced at centralized facilities. Therefore, we believe this Air Force concern alone should not deter centralization.

Although an indepth analysis of transportation needs to be made, options should be considered that could affect potential increased costs. For example, using the LOGAIR 1/ systems in the United States may alleviate the Air Force's transportation cost and availability concerns in the United States. Currently, the LOGAIR flights are flying at 70 percent capacity, thus the unused space is already paid for. Other options include using excess available capacity on military flights and the additional transportation space provided because, as the Pacific Air Force experienced, fewer items will require transportation to the depot.

In addition, we believe that significant cost savings in equipment, facilities, and personnel should be more than adequate to offset any additional costs for spare parts or transportation.

Equipment

Savings in equipment costs would be more than $56 million primarily by reducing the number of avionics shops. The Air Force is planning to buy approximately 36 avionics intermediate shops--each costing $8 million--to support repair of 1,388 F-16s. If shops were centralized in the United States and Europe, the Air Force could reduce its requirements by at least seven shops.

Additional savings are available, as reported in a June 1978 Air Force Logistics Management Center study, 2/ in jet engine, electrical, and environmental shops. The equipment

---

1/LOGAIR is an Air Force system for regular delivery of supply and maintenance items among bases in the continental United States using commercial contract aircraft.

2/USAFE-CILC Study-Weapon Applicability for USAFE CILC F-15, F-16, F-111 Report (AFLMC Study, June 15, 1978).

required in these shops for 72 aircraft would be sufficient for two or three times that number of aircraft in a centralized facility.

Personnel

Studies by GAO and others have shown that F-16 staffing can be reduced by centralizing F-16 intermediate maintenance. In our March 28, 1979, report, we noted that centralizing a wing (72 aircraft) of F-16s would reduce overhead personnel 53 percent and shop personnel 19 percent. Furthermore, centralizing the F-4 intermediate repair facilities has proven that personnel savings are possible. The official personnel records show that 27 spaces were saved in the F-4 program as a result of centralizing approximately 135 F-4s.

The June 1978 Air Force Logistics Management Center study revealed the following personnel savings possible in peacetime and wartime.

	No. of aircraft	F-16 Personnel Current planned base	Centralized facility	Potential reductions
Peacetime (note a)	96	277	240	37
Wartime (note b)	186	577	498	79

a/Projection of total staffing and deployment of F-16s in Europe for the fiscal year 1982 F-16 force.

b/Total staffing and aircraft available for deployment in fiscal year 1982.

Although exact savings cannot be predicted for the total F-16 force, the potential is significant. As shown above, reductions by just 37 and 79 personnel would produce yearly cost savings of approximately $740,000 and $1,580,000, respectively.

Facilities

The June 1978 Air Logistics Management Center study also reported that significant facility savings are available by centralizing. For example, although the number of aircraft for a centralized facility would increase by over 150 percent (72 to 186 aircraft), the additional facility square footage required would increase only by about 33 percent, as shown on the following page.

Maintenance activity	Facility size required	
	72 aircraft	186 aircraft (note a)
	(square feet)	
Avionics shops	15,888	32,688
Electrical system shop	1,176	1,676
Environmental shop	1,188	1,688
Pneudraulics shop	1,504	2,104
Jet engine intermedi-ate maintenance shop	18,640	18,640
Reparable asset control shop	10,000	10,000
Overhead space	7,230	7,230
Total facility size	55,626	74,026

a/Total aircraft available for deployment in fiscal year
 1982 as reported in the June 1978 Air Force Logistics
 Management Center study.

As shown above, each aircraft in a 72 F-16 wing requires
773 square feet of facility space. When the unit size increases to 186 aircraft, each additional aircraft over 72 requires only 161 square feet, resulting in a savings of 612
square feet per aircraft. On the basis of an average cost of
$60 per square foot, this would be $36,720. For the F-16,
fleet savings would be significant. For example, consolidating just three wings (216 of the 1,388 planned aircraft)
would save approximately $5.3 million.

System survivability

The Air Force has been concerned that a centralized
facility would be more vulnerable to enemy attack, thus, pos-
sibly disrupting the complete intermediate repair facility.
However, DOD studies point out that a centralized facility
would be less vulnerable. A February 1979 Defense Resource
Management study reported that removing the repair facility
from the immediate combat zone in the Pacific Air Force makes
it less vulnerable to direct attack. (Maintenance facilities
located at air bases are near runways and aircraft which are
primary targets.) An October 1979 Rand Corporation study also
said that centralizing intermediate repair facilities could
not be ruled out solely because of the resultant indirect
threat to support system survivability.

The Air Force is addressing the survivability/
vulnerability issue in its study on centralization to be completed in December 1980.

ADDITIONAL BENEFITS OF CENTRALIZATION

In addition to reducing logistics costs, centralized intermediate maintenance makes possible

--improved logistical support and

--better aircraft unit mobility.

Improved logistical support

Centralized intermediate maintenance facilities have
better opportunities than decentralized facilities to produce
high quality spare and repair parts as quickly as possible.
This happens primarily because personnel in a centralized
facility have the opportunity to specialize and to receive
more advanced training. As a result, personnel are more
highly trained and their work is of better quality, requiring
less depot repair.

The Pacific Air Force's experiences show that centralization can also help prevent inequities by providing a central
distribution and storage system with the oversight necessary
to send spare parts to units with the greatest needs. Under
decentralization, each operating unit controls its own level
of spare parts. Consequently, some commands may have excess
spare parts, while others have critical shortages and greater
needs.

Also, a centralized support facility will be able to
stock a greater range and depth of repair parts and enhance
its ability to cannibalize, thereby consolidating shortages on
fewer units. This increased level of spares helps reduce
base reparables being sent to depot for repair and results
in less aircraft downtime. For example, at the Pacific F-4
Centralized Intermediate Repair Facility, the "not reparable
this station" rates went down dramatically (about 20 percent),
the quality of the repair improved (above 30 percent), and
the total number of line replaceable units shipped to depot
for repair dropped by 50 percent. The F-16 program should be
able to reap similar benefits.

Centralization provides better
aircraft unit mobility

Centralization provides a tactical unit with greater flexi-
bility and mobility, because the tactical commander has no

responsibility managing and moving intermediate maintenance personnel, support equipment, and supplies. The February 1979 Defense Resource Management study reported that centralization would relieve an A-10 aircraft commander of the burden of housing, feeding, transporting, and managing approximately 100 personnel per squadron. Centralization would also reduce supplies and transportation by 1,300 pounds per day. By reducing the unit's responsibility for these support functions, it will be more mobile and ready for combat.

We believe similar savings should be available for the F-16. Also, the unit would not be concerned with transporting heavy intermediate maintenance equipment, making it easier to move as the situation demanded.

COOPERATION NEEDED TO PROVIDE EUROPEAN DEPOT REPAIR FOR U.S. F-16s

Although the United States is committed to using EPGs' depot support for the U.S. F-16s in Europe, little if any support will be available when the F-16 activates in Europe. If the Air Force expects to meet U.S. commitments, it must solve the problems preventing support from being available. Factors that must be examined include

--U.S. commitment to EPGs,

--inherent obstacles to using EPGs' support, and

--U.S. cost and readiness consequences.

U.S. commitment to EPGs

The Memorandum of Understanding between the United States and the EPGs contains the following commitment:

"The US Department of Defense, subject to congressional authorization and appropriations, will * * * utilize depot level maintenance and overhaul facilities established and funded by the European participating countries and industry maintenance facilities in these countries on a mutually agreed basis for maintenance and overhaul of USAF [United States Air Force] F-16 aircraft operated in Europe * * *."

The United States also committed itself and DOD to achieve a minimum offset level of 58 percent of the procurement costs for the EPGs' initial 348 F-16 aircraft procurement. Although depot repair value was not initially included in the 58-percent offset, an agreement reached in January 1980 now permits it. Currently, Air Force officials do not know

17

the F-16 depot repair offset potential, but previously they estimated it to be a maximum of $147 million between 1981 and 1986.

Although Air Force officials contend that they had always intended for EPGs to provide depot support of Air Force F-16s, the Air Force did not have time frames for EPG depot support in the F-16 ILS plan. In March 1980 the depot support equipment branch chief said the Air Force was developing the depot support plan.

Although a commitment exists, both the United States and the EPGs are waiting on each other to make the necessary decisions and commitments. For example, Air Force officials say they cannot count on EPGs doing depot repair until the EPGs establish and fund the maintenance repair facilities. Yet, the EPGs insist they cannot establish or fund the facilities until they have a U.S. repair commitment to justify their investments. As a result, the Air Force currently expects to have few, if any, EPG depot repair shops for U.S. F-16s when they activate in Europe in 1981.

Obstacles to using EPGs' support

Although the EPGs want to do depot repair work on our planes in Europe, many problems restrict their ability to do so. The EPGs' senior national representatives from Denmark, the Netherlands, and Norway expressed the following concerns:

--The actual Air Force decision to permit EPGs to do U.S. depot repairs was made too late to give the EPGs enough time to have depot repair facilities available when the aircraft begin arriving in 1981.

--Most of the EPGs' F-16 repair facilities are fully engaged in producing the airplane. They will not be able to accept much repair work until production contracts end.

--The United States restricts repair contracts to 1 year, with no guarantees for future repair work. This conflicts with the European hiring philosophy, which, in effect, says once hired always hired. Repair personnel can not be laid off at the end of a single year's contract. One-year contracts may make it extremely difficult to justify the capital expenditures necessary and to remain cost competitive.

--The United States has not established guidelines or plans for implementing the depot repair program.

--The Air Force has not provided the EPGs lists of F-16 reparables that would be available for depot repair, so they have no basis to begin planning.

In commenting on a draft of this report, Belgium said its industry would have the capability of doing depot repair work and would also be able to do so during the production process. It is Belgium policy to place 1 year repair contracts with no guarantees for future repair work, but with implicit extension of the contract associated with an annual termination clause. However, the Air Force has yet to contract with any of the EPGs for any F-16 depot repair.

Successful ILS planning requires the Air Force to be aware of and resolve these problems. If not resolved, European depot support will be delayed, the United States may not meet its Memorandum of Understanding commitments with the EPGs, and the uncertainty will make Air Force logistics planning difficult. Early solution of these problems can reduce Air Force requirements for support equipment, personnel, training, maintenance, and transportation.

Cost and readiness considerations

Overall, the Air Force believes the cost of EPG depot repair is comparable with U.S. repair costs. However, because the Air Force has not yet planned for EPG depot repair, it may be overbuying equipment for U.S. repair capabilities. Using EPG depot repair also should improve F-16 readiness in Europe.

The United States needs to make its decision concerning depot repair as quickly as possible to avoid purchasing excess equipment and supplies for repair work the EPGs may do in the future. For example, the Air Force purchased its depot-level avionics test equipment without considering potential depot repair to be done by the EPGs. As a result, the Air Force may have overstated its automatic test equipment requirements by $7 million. Air Force officials say that this equipment is now needed to supply the increased test time requirements to test other automatic equipment and to meet increased requirements resulting from engineering changes.

Air Force officials should reexamine the potential value, volume, and availability of EPG depot support before purchasing additional testing equipment. A reduction in test equipment would bring about a corresponding reduction in facilities and personnel if EPGs do this testing and repair.

19

EPG repairs should improve Air Force readiness. Air Force officials are evaluating the potential for increased readiness and believe that more serviceable equipment would be available since the lengthy depot repair turnaround time to the United States would be reduced.

UNNECESSARY PROCUREMENT OF F-16 AIRCRAFT
FOR BACKUP AIRCRAFT INVENTORY

Although the Air Force designed the F-16 aircraft to eliminate scheduled depot overhaul, it is still allowing for a 10-percent backup aircraft inventory, traditionally needed to draw from when regular aircraft must be modified or repaired in depot. To justify purchasing 110 F-16s--costing $1.4 billion--as backups, the Air Force cited the traditional 10-percent need. While some backup aircraft may be needed for the modification program, they should only be authorized after carefully considering units' needs. They should not be authorized merely because that is what was always done.

The F-16 was planned and designed to eliminate the need for planned depot overhaul. Organizational and intermediate maintenance will be done in the field, and only component parts needing depot-level repair will be removed and sent to depot for repair. The Air Force has developed new design features and adopted the reliability centered maintenance program (which monitors the condition of equipment) to help ensure maintenance will be done in the field. In spite of this, the F-16 is still using a 10-percent factor to compute backup aircraft inventory. Since the F-16 is not scheduled for periodic depot overhaul, the justification for 110 F-16s is questionable.

Pricing data given to the Congress in December 1979 indicates that each F-16 will cost about $12.6 million. In addition, sizable annual operating costs per aircraft are involved. Therefore, by reducing the F-16 backup inventory aircraft, the Air Force potentially could save $1.4 billion in procurement funds and sizable annual operating funds.

According to the Air Force, some of the pipeline aircraft are needed as substitutes for aircraft undergoing modifications. However, the number of F-16 modifications, and therefore the need for the pipeline aircraft, is unknown.

If modifications indeed represent a sizable workload, then the Air Force should carefully assess how many aircraft really are needed for substitutes. This assessment should also take into account how much of this workload is peacetime workload and how quickly aircraft in the depot would be needed for deployment. Only after these questions are answered should a decision be made to determine if substitute or maintenance float aircraft are indeed needed and, if so, how many.

We also recommended reducing backup inventory for the A-10 aircraft in a previous report. 1/ In discussing that report, Air Force officials generally felt that the additional aircraft were needed. However, they said a study effort was starting to determine aircraft requirements, including how percentages for backup aircraft are developed.

CONCLUSIONS

Centralizing intermediate maintenance, rather than having each unit independently support its own aircraft, is a concept that has proven effective for other aircraft weapon systems. While centralization can benefit a program, early planning and action are imperative to take advantage of those benefits.

Using centralized intermediate maintenance for the F-16 would result in reduced equipment, personnel, and facility costs and improve operational effectiveness. The longer the Air Force waits to centralize, the fewer the benefits will be. For example, the Air Force must order some of the major repair and test equipment 3 years in advance, and if planning is not done early, this equipment will already be contracted for and the important advantage of reducing equipment purchases will be lost.

Although committed by the Memorandum of Understanding to having the EPGs do depot repair for U.S. F-16s in Europe, the Air Force is moving slowly. The Air Force has not determined where or by whom the F-16 depot repair will be provided. As a result, only limited support will be available when U.S. F-16s activate in Europe. Also, the Air Force may have overbought equipment for U.S. depot needs. If the Air Force does not use the EPGs for depot repair, it may not meet the Memorandum of Understanding commitments.

Although the Air Force traditionally provides a 10-percent backup aircraft inventory, the need for it is questionable for the F-16. The F-16 was designed to eliminate planned depot maintenance and overhaul, and the extent of substitute aircraft needed for the F-16 modification program is not known. By reducing the backup inventory, the Air Force can save up to $1.4 billion.

1/"Unnecessary Procurement of A-10 Aircraft for Depot Maintenance Floats" (LCD-79-431, Sept. 6, 1979).

AGENCY COMMENTS AND OUR EVALUATION

DOD made no specific comments on our recommendations concerning (1) accelerating negotiations with EPGs to determine if and how much U.S. depot repair will be done in Europe and (2) reexamining the potential value, volume, and availability of EPG depot support before purchasing additional test equipment. We also gave the EPGs an opportunity to review a draft of this report. Denmark, the Netherlands, and Norway had no substantial comments, and Belgium's comment on its capability of doing depot work was added to page 19.

DOD disagreed with our recommendations that the Air Force (1) centralize F-16 intermediate maintenance and (2) reexamine the need for backup aircraft inventory. Concerning centralized maintenance, DOD said that centralization of F-16 maintenance in Europe is not likely to be more effective or efficient than under its current logistics structure. However, to assure that the current logistics structure is still valid, the Air Force is reexamining the centralized F-16 intermediate maintenance concept.

DOD's arguments about added costs and vulnerability are already addressed in this chapter and the information should be evaluated in DOD's current study. On the basis of data available, we still believe that centralization is a feasible, cost-effective option.

DOD disagreed with our recommendation on reducing backup aircraft inventory. DOD stated that any attempt to zero in on a single, "correct" factor for backup aircraft inventory does not recognize the real world uncertainties. According to DOD, the 10-percent factor historically has been accurate for tactical fighter aircraft and should continue to be used for the F-16 procurement. We do not advocate a single correct factor as DOD implies, and we recognize that some backup aircraft may be needed. However, we believe that since the F-16 was planned and designed to eliminate the need for planned depot overhaul, the need for backup aircraft should be reduced sharply compared to historical needs. At a per aircraft cost of $12.6 million, the need for each backup aircraft should be carefully reevaluated.

RECOMMENDATIONS

We recommend that the Secretary of Defense direct the Air Force to

--centralize F-16 intermediate maintenance;

--accelerate negotiations with the EPGs to determine if
  and how much U.S. depot repair will be done in Europe
  to meet the Memorandum of Understanding commitments;

--reexamine the potential value, volume, and availability
  of EPG depot support before purchasing additional test
  equipment; and

--reexamine the need for backup aircraft inventory.

CHAPTER 4

TRAINING EQUIPMENT: AN INTEGRAL

PART OF THE F-16 PROGRAM

The ILS plan for training and training devices is supposed to define what is needed to support these areas through all phases of the F-16 program. The essential elements for support are provided. However, Air Force logistics planners should consider other alternatives in both the maintenance crew and the pilot training programs.

THE SIMULATED AIRCRAFT MAINTENANCE
TRAINER IS INEFFECTIVE

The simulated aircraft maintenance trainer (SAMT) offers the Air Force a new maintenance training concept that potentially has several advantages. However, experience with the first of three SAMT groups (10 trainers per group) under contract for $3 million each has not confirmed that the concept is feasible. Further research is needed. Also, because the Air Force underestimated the time needed to develop this trainer--allowing only 1 year for development and production-- it now finds the simulated maintenance training program has to be changed to work around its limited capabilities.

The Air Force did not provide
an adequate development period

SAMT is composed of 10 trainers which simulate the mechanical and electrical operations of the major aircraft subsystems. A minicomputer controls each trainer.

The Air Force cites several advantages to this approach over the use of conventional trainers, which are built using actual aircraft hardware and cost more than $10 million each. These advantages include the reduced need for training on operational aircraft, a lower cost to buy and alter equipment, and the ability to program faults into the simulator without physically altering any hardware on the training device.

Because the Air Force planned for almost immediate use of the simulator, it did not adequately assess the complexity of the simulator's development and the problems that then existed. For example:

--The software had not been developed.

--The contractor had limited experience in software.

24

--Development of the aircraft was just beginning, and
  therefore, it could be subjected to continual changes.

--The initial requirements submitted to the contractor
  were unclear at the time the contract was awarded.

The Air Force, by not thoroughly understanding the complexity of developing this simulator, believed the contractor
could meet the 1-year delivery schedule. Thus, it did not
provide alternative training plans. Air Force officials said
that three of the four contractors who bid said that they
could deliver on time.

Costs have escalated as a result of this limited development effort. Continual modifications in aircraft design have
required changes in the simulator. The current SAMT group
cost is approximately $3 million.

The Air Force did not consider
training alternatives

Although the Air Force researched the benefits of simulation over conventional hardware before deciding to buy the
simulator, it did not adequately consider training alternatives in the event of delivery delay.

The F-16 training plan revolved around extensive use of
the simulator at each field training detachment. Course outlines and lesson plans described in detail the course objectives which must be met through the SAMT's use. None of the
plans available gave contingency procedures should problems
cause delays in simulator availability. Because it did not
consider this possibility, the Air Force had to work around
the problem when it occurred by (1) rewriting course outlines
and lesson plans, (2) retraining previously trained students,
(3) increasing the use of actual aircraft for training, and
(4) retaining contractor personnel to make up for shortages
of trained maintenance personnel. Had the Air Force had contingency plans, course objectives may have been met with less
disruption to training programs.

The simulator has not met training
objectives, but it has potential

When the SAMTs began arriving at Hill Air Force Base in
September 1979, about 1 year after schedule, their condition
was unsatisfactory. The Air Training Command refused to for-
mally accept them because of their condition and because three
trainers were being delayed indefinitely. However, an interim
acceptance was signed so the simulators could be used
immediately.

Although the simulator is being used in the maintenance training program, it has not provided the support it was designed for. Instructors cited several serious technical problems as the cause. For example, many instructors felt that the simulator's troubleshooting capabilities, considered its most important function, were insufficient. According to instructors, two trainers were totally incapable of teaching troubleshooting.

The Air Force estimates that it will need seven complete SAMT groups to accommodate the planned 1,388 aircraft. The decision to buy the remaining four SAMT groups will depend on the total aircraft purchased, the cost of the SAMT, and also on the training value of the current three. Some field training detachment and field training group instructors and Air Training Command officials felt that the simulators on hand, although not working up to par, had instructional value and could provide substantial savings once design problems were solved. Without a dedicated effort to validate the feasibility and training value of the SAMT, however, expectations for the program may never come to pass. Such an effort is also significant because Air Force officials said they are considering simulators of this type for other aircraft systems, including the F-15, F-111, and A-10.

PILOT TRAINING EQUIPMENT
IS STILL BEING DEVELOPED

Portions of the F-16 pilot training equipment are still being developed. However, since Air Force planners have already decided to install a complete pilot trainer complex (a weapon system trainer) at each active F-16 base (and an additional one at each of two training bases), at a unit cost of $65 million, the Air Force could be buying more training equipment than is needed. For example, although the Air Force projects that pilots will use the weapon system trainer 35.5 hours every 6 months, 65 percent of this projection (approximately 24 hours) deals with new areas of simulation on which no historical usage data exists. When actual usage data is obtained, trainer capacity may be such where two or more bases sharing a single training facility may be more economical. Another option would be to use less than a complete weapon system trainer at the same location. This is the current plan for Air Force Guard and Reserve F-16 simulation training. Because of the substantial cost per unit, the Air Force should consider these alternatives rather than purchasing a complete weapon system trainer for every base.

The weapon system trainer consists of two operational flight trainers, a system that visually duplicates flight conditions, a digital system, and two electronic warfare trainers. According to design goals, the weapon system trainer will be able to simulate practically any fighter mission, including emergencies and the pilot being able to see an attacking missile. The trainer will also be able to train two pilots at once.

Training on the first operational flight trainer is scheduled to begin in May 1981. However, the visual portion is still in development. A decision to buy one of two prototype visual systems will be made in April 1984. Meanwhile, the complete weapon system trainer is planned for every operational U.S. Air Force F-16 base. According to Air Force officials, having a complete weapon system trainer at every base would enhance readiness, since pilots would not have to be away from their duty stations training at another base. However, since projected simulator usage is only 71 hours a year per pilot, it does not appear that this would cause significant problems.

Because they do not yet know the capacity of the visual system, Air Force officials said they cannot say exactly how often it will be used. The design goal is for the system to be used 16 hours a day, 6 days a week. Actual capacity will not be determined until April 1984.

CONCLUSIONS

Because the Air Force has never used maintenance training simulators, logistics planners should have considered some alternative training methods before purchasing the simulators. This would have allowed enough time to design and test the system adequately and given the aircraft time to stabilize before the first training units went into production. Simulators developed design and production problems, resulting in substituted training methods. Although the Air Force claims that it still was able to provide quality training, it could have avoided the added expense of working around the problems with the trainers. Since simulators still have operational problems and not all have been delivered, the Air Force should resolve the operational uncertainties of the simulators and develop contingency plans for training in case simulator delivery is further delayed.

According to Air Force officials, having complete weapon system trainers at every base would enhance readiness, since pilots would not have to be away from their duty stations training at another base. However, since projected simulator usage is only 71 hours a year per pilot, this does not appear to be a significant factor. Rather, we believe that because of the significant weapon system trainer cost--$65 million per unit--Air Force planners should obtain actual usage data

27

before buying a weapon system trainer for each active base. Once equipment capabilities and capacities are compared to actual needs, it may be more cost effective to have some bases share equipment. Also, because weapon system trainers are comprised of different components that can provide independent training, but at reduced levels, the Air Force could use less than a complete weapon system trainer at some locations. This is what is used on other aircraft and what is being planned for the Air Force Guard and Reserve F-16 simulator training.

AGENCY COMMENTS AND OUR EVALUATION

DOD made no specific comments on our recommendations concerning resolving the operational uncertainties of the SAMT program and providing contingency plans in case delivery of the SAMTs is delayed further.

DOD stated that centralization of F-16 weapon system training devices to a few selected sites is contrary to the Air Force's position to collocate simulators with operational and training units whenever possible. DOD also felt that, based on projected aircrew usage, a weapon system trainer is required at every F-16 base.

We did not specify that trainers be consolidated at a "few" selected sites. Rather, we pointed out that the decision for each base to have a weapon system trainer should be subjected to a cost/benefit analysis. For example, although the actual base locations are classified, two bases are less than 500 miles apart. Also, because most of the training areas are new to simulation, DOD's projected usage data may change once actual experience is obtained.

Considering the proximity of some bases, unproven usage data, and the high unit cost of the weapon system trainer, we believe the Air Force's position of trainer collocation with operational and training units "whenever possible" should be reevaluated.

RECOMMENDATIONS

We recommend that the Secretary of Defense direct the Air Force to

--promptly resolve the operational uncertainties of the SAMT program,

--provide contingency plans in case delivery of the SAMTs is delayed further, and

--assess the cost/benefit of buying a weapon system
   trainer for every F-16 base.

CHAPTER 5

TECHNICAL ORDERS DEVELOPED LATE

Although the Air Force must receive fully tested technical orders before it can do maintenance work, many F-16 technical orders were not usable by the Air Force until well after aircraft were delivered. Technical orders, a major part of the ILS element "technical data," are written instructions for Air Force personnel explaining how to install, operate, and repair aircraft equipment. Having technical orders concurrent with aircraft and related equipment is an important objective of integrated logistics management.

Contractor and Air Force controls over testing of technical orders have been inadequate, causing serious quality problems and postponing Air Force maintenance. Also, to correct inaccurate orders and to purchase interim contractor maintenance support until orders are available for Air Force mechanics add additional cost to the estimated $200 million required to develop, test, and maintain orders.

To combat technical order problems, the Air Force has established special technical order review groups, increased the technical order staff, and attempted to coordinate orders with the using command to correct deficiencies on existing orders. Further improvements are needed for the remaining F-16 technical order development and testing--this should lower costs and improve weapon system support.

VALIDATION AND VERIFICATION PROCESS

Before the Air Force accepts technical orders, they must be reviewed to ensure their usability and compliance with military specifications. There are two stages of review: validation and verification. Validation is a process by which the contractor tests the proposed maintenance and operating procedures for accuracy, adequacy, completeness, and comparability with the applicable military specification.

Once the technical orders are validated, the Air Force verifies the procedures in an operational environment to assure the technical orders are clear, logical, and adequate for operating and maintaining the equipment.

IMPROVED QUALITY POSSIBLE

Because many of the complex F-16 technical orders--for intermediate and depot maintenance--remain to be developed, the Air Force has an excellent opportunity to improve order quality. This will, however, require emphasis on technical order development.

Air Force regulations state that technical orders must be delivered before or concurrently with the delivery of equipment. However, our review of technical order management, development, and testing processes indicates that this is not the case. The result has been poor quality orders with time consuming changes causing delays. As a result, the Air Force has been forced to buy unplanned contractor maintenance support and, thus far, has obligated approximately $2.5 million for such support.

Improvements in staffing and the validation/verification process are needed to improve the technical order program and timeliness of order delivery.

Better staffing needed for technical order program

Air Force officials repeatedly cited three reasons why staffing for technical order management, development, and testing received little emphasis: inexperienced personnel, inadequate staffing early in the program, and frequent management turnover.

Although the shortage of trained personnel is well recognized, the Air Force has no system for developing an experienced technical staff. There is no formal technical order training program; any training is obtained on the job.

In the critical period when the initial F-16 technical orders were being defined, placed under contract, and developed, the program had four managers in 3 years; none had any technical order acquisition background. Air Force officials said the lack of adequate staffing was magnified because they had to develop specifications for a completely new organizational maintenance technical order concept, called the Maintenance Integrated Data Access System. In addition, Air Force officials were also developing the technical orders concurrently with an accelerated, ever changing aircraft development program.

Inadequate technical order validation/verification

Only after repeated Air Force complaints of poor quality technical orders was it discovered that, although required by regulation, some technical orders delivered were not contractor validated. The Air Force representatives at the contractor plant estimated that approximately 10 percent of the organizational level technical orders were delivered unvalidated. Representatives believed they were not required to observe contractor validations, although an agreement between the F-16 Systems Program Office and Air Force testing team required it. This incomplete contractor testing and insufficient Air Force observations led to some of the poor quality.

The Air Force has improved the development and validation processes by increasing the number of Air Force reviews of technical orders. This method will ensure that the contractor fully understands Air Force requirements. In addition, the Air Force is complying with requirements that it observe contractor validations. However, further improvements are possible. Comprehensive inspections and in-process reviews before verification would also improve quality. Problems identified during verification should be reduced, and the contractor would receive increased feedback on what the Air Force wants. This would also reduce costs for initial changes which have been $7 million through May 1980.

Greater inter-Air Force understanding could improve verification

The ILS concept calls for the interaction of user and support organizations to achieve a well supported weapon system. Improvements are needed in technical order development. The fragmented assignments of responsibility for production and testing of technical orders make interaction important in the F-16 program.

Although the technical order manager is responsible for completing verification on time, he has no control over the assets needed for the job. Tactical Air Command, the user of the orders, controls assets and actually performs the verification. While the command claims verification is given top priority, technical order managers noted a distinct lack of dedicated assets--particularly aircraft and knowledgeable personnel--and little emphasis on prompt verification.

CONCLUSIONS

Technical orders are not being completed as quickly as they could be, and despite delays, they are often of poor quality. This indicates that the ILS plan is not functioning smoothly, even after some Air Force improvements. Strict management of the plan is lacking, some existing systems and procedures are inadequate, and coordination is ineffective. These problems will not be solved easily, but the effort will be justified by cutting the costs of developing upcoming technical orders. Because these orders are now being prepared, Air Force action is needed as soon as possible.

RECOMMENDATIONS

    We recommend that the Secretary of Defense direct the
Air Force to

    --provide sufficient resources to the validation and
      verification of technical orders to eliminate problems
      created by lateness and poor quality and

    --improve current systems of quality assurance by re-
      quiring more frequent comprehensive inspections and
      in-process reviews before delivering technical orders
      to the Air Force for verification.

AGENCY COMMENTS

    DOD made no specific comments on our recommendations
other than to say that the Air Force previously has identified
the F-16 logistics areas discussed as requiring management
attention.

CHAPTER 6

F-16 SUPPLY SUPPORT COULD IMPROVE

The F-16 supply support plan is supposed to provide for proper levels of supply. However, spare parts for the aircraft engine are in short supply, and adequate funding is not available for spare parts kits used to support those aircraft first deployed during wartime.

To meet its mission requirements, a major weapon system depends on the availability of supplies at the time and place they are needed. Supply support is an essential element of logistics which ensures prompt provisioning, distribution, and restocking of spares, repair parts, and special supplies.

SOME ENGINE PARTS ARE IN SHORT SUPPLY

The Air Force is having problems maintaining adequate levels of spare parts for the F-100 engine, which is used in both the F-15 and F-16 aircraft. Generally, the Air Force recognizes this problem.

Shortages are occurring for approximately 2 percent (60 to 100 items) of the F-100 spare parts. This percentage may seem small, but it could have a serious impact on aircraft readiness. As of November 1979, an above average number of engines--23.2 percent--were not available because of supply problems. An Air Force official felt that a 10-percent goal would be reasonable. These figures cover engines for both the F-15 and F-16 because the data is not kept separately.

According to Air Force officials, the two primary reasons for the shortages are that not enough spare parts were ordered and the spare parts on order did not arrive on schedule.

Not enough spare parts ordered

Officials stated that ordering parts for this engine is an extremely complex task. Because the engine is relatively new and immature, unexpected failures commonly occur. For this reason, usage or replacement rates for parts often change. Sometimes this creates the need for items which, due to long procurement leadtimes, are not readily available and could not have been foreseen as needed. Parts shortages, of course, are the end result.

When the Air Force began ordering parts for the F-100 engine, it started with usage factors provided by the contractor, Pratt and Whitney, and with data collected from the F-100 engine used on the twin-engined F-15. As the engine gained flying experience and testing in the single-engined F-16, problems developed which caused increased usage in some parts. As a result, quantities initially projected and ordered proved to be insufficient.

For example, the burnout rate for hot section parts has proven to be much higher than the contractor predicted. The increased usage of these parts, combined with long leadtimes for hot section parts, left the Air Force with a serious parts shortage.

A change in engine maintenance schedule also complicated spare parts forecasting. Previously, engines were inspected after 1,250 cycles (hours) of operation. However, since the F-100 engine was experiencing a series of mechanical problems, the Air Force decided to change the inspection schedule to 900 cycles. Unexpected wear on some parts was discovered, which required adjusting the usage factors.

The Air Force could not prevent the spares shortage. Now that the engine has gained flying experience and the usage factors for parts are better known, however, the Air Force can use this information to more accurately calculate spare parts requirements.

Contractors not meeting delivery schedules

The contractors' failure to meet delivery schedules has become a serious problem in spare parts acquisition. Air Force officials indicate that it has become common for suppliers to miss delivery dates by months, or even years. The causes include such things as material shortages, limitations of industrial capacity, and strikes. Failures of small businesses have also been a factor.

Material shortages have posed a major problem, especially in those parts made from exotic, lightweight metals. Many of the parts in the F-100 use these metals. Without them, production is delayed; in turn, delivery is delayed.

The industrial capacity of the United States has declined to a point where a few people serve many customers. This is especially true in the casting, forging, and bearing industries, which are vital to jet engine production. When the Government experiences long delays because these industries cannot keep up with demand, it often has no alternative other than to wait its turn.

The Air Force estimates that, due to a strike at an engine subcontractor's plant, 5 of the 95 F-16s delivered as of April 1980 will be without engines temporarily. According to Air Force officials, the number of F-16s without engines has been reduced recently because Pratt and Whitney has increased engine production and some spare engines will be used in production aircraft.

First F-16 fighter wing short engine spares

The 388th Tactical Fighter Wing, the first and only F-16 wing designated so far, has been short engine spares, which could increase maintenance work and reduce the number of flyable aircraft. Some Air Force officials believe the engine spares shortage is becoming extremely critical.

To meet its planned flying hours, the 388th is compensating for the spare parts shortage by dismantling engines for the parts, which results in extra maintenance and handling procedures. In December 1979 the 388th informed Tactical Air Command headquarters that the nonavailability of a certain engine sensor would increase its maintenance hours and the number of aircraft out of commission. To lessen these problems, the Tactical Air Command is considering extending the time between required replacement of certain parts by 25 hours of flying time.

ALTERNATIVE TO THE F-100 ENGINE

If its proposed alternative engine to the F-14 and F-16 aircraft has problems similar to the present engine, the Air Force may increase rather than decrease its logistics costs.

Because of possible problems with the F-100 engine, the Air Force decided to develop an alternative replacement engine. In March 1979 General Electric was awarded a 30-month contract as part of a cooperative plan between the Air Force and Navy for development of the F-101DFE engine for possible use in the Navy's F-14 and the Air Force's F-16. The services plan to spend $93 million for this 30-month effort.

We believe the F-101DFE program is at least as uncertain of producing a production engine with enhanced operability and supportability characteristics as the F-100 improvement program. 1/ This is due simply to the differences in the two engines' stages of development. The F-100 engine will have

_____

1/"Is the Joint Air Force/Navy Alternate Engine Program Workable? GAO Thinks Not As Presently Structured" (PSAD-80-40, May 9, 1980).

36

accumulated 1 million flying hours in 1981 and will be reaching maturity in 1983. Conversely, the F-101DFE will have accumulated only about 1,700 ground test hours and 200 engine flying hours in 1981 when the decision is to be made on whether to continue the program into full-scale development.

Air Force officials cited the short development period for the F-100 as part of the reason for its early performance problems, which caused a strain on spare parts. The Commander of the Air Force Systems Command said that he strongly believes that future engine development must be initiated well ahead of the aircraft it will power. Given the short development period allotted the F-101DFE engine, the Air Force may experience similar support problems with it. In addition, supporting two different engines for the same aircraft may cause additional logistics problems.

SPARES FOR FIRST-DEPLOYED F-16s
MAY NOT BE AVAILABLE

The number of F-16s that could carry out their missions in time of conflict could be very small, because sufficient war reserve spare parts may not be available. Funds originally intended for war reserve spares were diverted to other programs.

Generally, Air Force squardons deploy with enough spare parts to meet their wartime needs for the 30 days before the logistics system can provide the needed parts. The interim parts are referred to as either base-level, self-sufficiency spares kits, or war-readiness spares kits.

The base-level spares kits consist of enough components and subcomponents to cover the increased level of wartime operations for a specified period of time. The 24- and 48- aircraft squadron base-level spares kits cost about $17 million and $30 million, respectively.

War-readiness spares kits are primarily composed of components needed to support a unit after it deploys to a new location in wartime. An F-16 war-readiness spares kit costs about $40 million for a 48-aircraft squadron.

Insufficient funding for war-readiness spares

The first F-16 wing will be available for deployment in January 1981, but war-readiness spares may not be available. This is because money set aside to buy war-readiness kits was diverted to the peacetime spares replenishment program.

Why was the money diverted? Peacetime spares were out of stock because the estimated replacement rate had been too low for new weapon systems, including the F-16. When this happens, the normal procedure is to use aircraft spares funds (one fund for both peacetime replenishment and wartime reserves) for the higher priority program. Peacetime operating stock is given the first priority; war-readiness spares, second.

According to Air Force officials, of the $49.5 million of fiscal year 1978 war-readiness funds, $35.4 million was diverted to make up for the fund shortage in the peacetime spares program. Also, acccording to Air Force officials, fiscal year 1979 war-readiness funds were also diverted. For fiscal year 1980, the Air Force is in the process of providing $87 million to the war-readiness spares program. However, these funds will be used to support the President's Persian Gulf Rapid Deployment Force, and, since the F-16 is not a part of this force, it will not receive any of the funds for its war-readiness spares.

Longer leadtimes for spares and higher inflation rates than anticipated also affected peacetime and wartime spares replenishment. The leadtime for spares had increased as a result of (1) limited industry capability to meet both defense and civilian aircraft demand and (2) a shortage of critical metals needed in the manufacturing of certain airraft components. Also, an uncontrollable but contributing factor to the eroding Air Force spares funds was the higher than anticipated inflation rates. For example, 6.5 percent was budgeted for inflation in the fiscal year 1979 aircraft spares replenishment program. However, the actual rate was nearly three times more than anticipated.

CONCLUSIONS

Some F-100 engine parts are in short supply, a condition which could mean that F-16s would not be ready to go to war. The problem was caused primarily by the Air Force underestimating the spares needed and by contractors not meeting their delivery schedules. These spares shortages must be eliminated to ensure the aircraft's combat readiness.

The Air Force awarded a contract for development of an engine, the F-101DFE, that could be used as an alternative to the F-100 engine. Given the short development period alloted to the F-101DFE engine, the Air Force may experience support and development problems similar to those in the F-100 engine program.

Spares for the first-deployed F-16s may not be available because war-readiness spares funds have been diverted to other programs. This spares shortage could affect the F-16's ability to carry out its mission in time of conflict.

AGENCY COMMENTS AND OUR EVALUATION

We proposed that the Air Force establish a separate budget fund for F-16 war-readiness spares. DOD disagreed. It said a separate fund would eliminate the Air Force's ability to manage the obligation and expenditure of spares dollars based on actual usage experience. Therefore, we have dropped the proposal.

DOD stated that the current system is flexible enough to respond to peacetime operational needs and war-readiness requirements as a total replenishment spares program. The fact remains, however, that spares may not be available when the first F-16s are deployed. Action is needed to get war-readiness spares into the system as soon as possible.

RECOMMENDATION

We recommend that the Secretary of Defense direct the Air Force to establish a timetable for F-16s to get war-readiness spares into the system for deployment.

CHAPTER 7

BETTER PLANNING NEEDED FOR FACILITIES

ILS planning for F-16 facilities does not provide the assurances which ILS plans should provide. DOD guidance calls for ILS planning which assures that facilities are available when needed. The ILS plan is also to be a dynamic, comprehensive plan for implementing the logistics concepts, techniques, and policies necessary to assure the effective economic support of a system during its life cycle. The F-16 ILS plan does not include the time needed to design and fabricate mobile shelters. Also, the plan has not been updated to show the new leadtimes needed to build facilities at bases getting the F-16.

As a result, the F-16 may have difficulty carrying out its fighting mission overseas, and some of the facilities at new F-16 bases are marginal.

PROTECTIVE SHELTERS MAY NOT BE AVAILABLE WHEN NEEDED

Shelters or other means of protecting the avionics intermediate maintenance equipment from the environment may be unavailable when needed. Air Force plans call for the F-16 avionics intermediate shop equipment to be ready for mobilization 7 days after the aircraft are deployed overseas, which may be as early as 1981. However, according to the F-16 Systems Program Office manager, the shelter is at least 2 years away from completion.

The purpose of the shelter is to provide a controlled environment for the avionics equipment, which has specific temperature, humidity, and power requirements and needs a smooth and level surface, a clean environment, and security for classified items. The equipment was designed to withstand temperatures from 10 to 35 degrees Centigrade, altitudes up to 6,000 feet, and humidity from 5 to 80 percent. 1/

A System Program Office official stated that interim measures, such as portable air-conditioning units being

---

1/In addition, the Electrical Standard Set which supports the avionics intermediate shop equipment has a recommended humidity range of 15 to 55 percent. When necessary, this range can be exceeded; however, limitations prevent calibration measurements from being valid in certain instances.

40

installed in the equipment, could be used to protect avionics equipment if shelters are not ready, and that temperature would not significantly affect the $8 million equipment for at least several months. However, Tactical Air Command officials indicated that, since the aircraft may be deployed in areas without the necessary environmentally controlled characteristics, the lack of a shelter could reduce aircraft readiness. According to a contractor representative, the avionics intermediate shop equipment automatically shuts down between 90 and 96 degrees Fahrenheit to protect itself from damage.

ILS PLAN SHOULD BE UPDATED

The July 1978 ILS plan contains dates when surveys, funding, and construction should be completed for the first operational and training bases during fiscal years 1976 through 1980. The plan was never updated to contain milestones for later bases. It also refers primarily to the use of minor construction funding, a procedure which was effectively eliminated in October 1978. These problems could cause delays in activating bases and, when bases are activated, could cause base facilities to be marginal.

New construction funding procedures
not recognized in plan

When construction funding procedures changed, the ILS plan was never updated to show that construction would take longer. The Congress changed procedures, effective October 1, 1978, so that all construction relating to a new aircraft at a base would be included in one project. This could have the effect of making the cost estimate for a new aircraft site more credible. Since $500,000 is now the dividing line between minor and major construction program projects, F-16 type construction projects come under the more time consuming major construction procedures. Air Force officials estimate that 36 to 42 months are required from start to finish on major construction projects, as compared to 18 months for a minor construction project. The ILS plan was never updated to refer to the increased use of the more time consuming major construction procedures.

Basing and funding leadtimes in conflict

Due to long funding leadtimes, ILS planners need to be more concerned in making basing decisions. When the Air Force selects a base for new aircraft stationing or changes a base selection, it must do so in sufficient time to allow

41

for funding leadtimes. An Air Force official stated that basing decisions sometimes change because of factors beyond their control, such as budget decisions, strikes, environmental impacts, and foreign military sales and associated training.

Planning for facilities to be available when needed is very difficult when base locations change. This happened with the F-16 basing schedule. Luke Air Force Base was selected in 1975 as the second base to get F-16s in January 1980. In 1978, when German Air Force training on the F-104 (which was to be phased out of Luke by fiscal year 1981) was extended through 1983, Luke was rejected as the second F-16 base, and MacDill Air Force Base was selected with the site activation date remaining at January 1, 1980. Major construction projects were started for MacDill in late 1978.

Air Force facilities planners consider MacDill facilities marginal, and they will remain so until the major construction projects started in 1980 are completed in 1981. Temporary measures will provide F-16 support; however, an Air Force official stated that conditions will be less than ideal. Fortunately, the dollar effect of the delay will be minimal because the F-16 is replacing the F-4 and most facilities differ just in the square footage required. For example, the ammunition maintenance shop for the F-16 requires 3,975 square feet versus the 2,370 square feet required for the F-4.

The conflict between the time required for facility construction and last-minute basing decisions may be a problem because adequate facilities may not be available in time for base activation. We believe the Air Force logistics planners should recognize the leadtimes required to ensure availability of facilities for future F-16 base activations.

CONCLUSIONS

DOD guidance states that support planning should assure that facilities are available when needed. The ability of the operating forces and supporting activities to carry out their missions could depend on the adequacy of facilities provided when the equipment is provided. Further guidance states that the ILS plan should consider the dates of need and construction program leadtimes.

Thus far, the objective of integrated support planning for F-16 facilities is marginally being met. Interim measures are being considered for the avionics intermediate shop equipment deployment and are being used at MacDill Air Force Base before military construction program projects can be completed.

If Air Force planners had followed DOD guidance to have the ILS plan as a dynamic, comprehensive way to carry out the logistics concept, facility problems could have at least been highlighted for quick solution. Without the addition of milestones, or the plan being updated, other less easily solvable problems may escape management attention. Furthermore, because the lack of mobile shelters may affect readiness, their completion should be accelerated, at least in those places where interim measures may not protect equipment adequately.

RECOMMENDATIONS

We recommend that the Secretary of Defense direct the Air Force to

- --accelerate completion of the mobile shelters as necessary to ensure protection of maintenance equipment when the F-16s are deployed and

- --update the ILS plan to recognize leadtimes required to ensure availability of facilities to support aircraft.

AGENCY COMMENTS

DOD made no specific comments on our recommendations other than to say that the Air Force previously has identified the F-16 logistics areas discussed as requiring management attention.

ASSISTANT SECRETARY OF DEFENSE

WASHINGTON D C 20301

MANPOWER
RESERVE AFFAIRS
AND LOGISTICS

June 16, 1980

Mr. R. W. Gutmann
Director, Logistics and
   Communications Division
U.S. General Accounting Office
Washington, D.C. 20548

Dear Mr. Gutmann:

This is in reply to your letter dated 8 May 1980 to the Secretary of Defense
regarding your draft report on "F-16 Integrated Logistics Support: Still Time
to Consider Alternative Plans and Save Money" (OSD Case #5435).

The report addresses several areas of the F-16 logistics program that have previously
been identified by the Air Force as requiring management attention. However, there
are four recommendations that require comment. These recommendations are:

   a. Centralizing F-16 intermediate maintenance in Europe and in the United
States

   b. Eliminating or reducing backup aircraft inventory

   c. Assessing the feasibility and cost/benefit of buying fewer than one
Weapon Systems Trainer for each F-16 base

   d. Establishing a separate budget fund for F-16 war-readiness spares

Centralization of F-16 maintenance in Europe is unlikely to be more effective or
efficient than our current logistics structure. Centralized intermediate maintenance requires assured transportation, additional pipeline spares, and ample
maintenance facilities at the central location. All three factors add considerable
costs to the F-16 support program and would become lucrative targets in time of
war. Loss of the assured transportation pipeline, or centralized facility would
adversely impact our combat units' capability to conduct their wartime mission.
However to assure that the current logistics structure is still valid, the Air Force
is in the process of reexamining the centralized F-16 intermediate maintenance concept.

Reduction or elimination of backup aircraft inventory (BAI) has been a continuing
subject of discussion with GAO over the past several years, first with the F-15,
subsequently the A-10, and currently the F-16. As we have stated in the past the
10% BAI has been and continues to be a good planning factor for the maintenance
backup portion of the total buy. Any attempt to zero-in on a single, "correct"

44

factor for BAI does not recognize the real world uncertainties of depot modification programs, analytical conditions inspections, structural integrity programs,
and crash/battle damage repair. The 10% BAI factor has been historically accurate
for our tactical fighter aircraft and should continue to be used for the F-16 procurement.

Centralization of F-16 Weapon System training devices to a few selected sites is
contrary to the Air Force practice to collocate simulators with operational and
training units whenever possible. Flight simulators are an integral part of each
unit's training and flying safety program as well as being essential to our efforts
to reduce operational and maintenance costs by replacing flying hours with simulator
time. Centralization would require frequent aircrew TDY that reduces each unit's
ability to meet local training, alert, and combat commitments. Based on projected
aircrew usage, one F-16 Weapon System Trainer is required at each location.

Establishing a separarate budget fund for F-16 war-readiness spares would eliminate
the Air Force's ability to manage the obligation and expenditure of spares dollars
based on actual usage experience in 11 weapon systems. The current system is
flexible enough to respond to peacetime operational needs and war-readiness requirements as a total replenishment spares program.

We appreciate this opportunity to comment about your draft report and further wish
to express our pleasure with the professionalism with which your auditors partici-
pated in our joint review.

Sincerely,

Robert B. Pirie, Jr.
Assistant Secretary of Defense
(Manpower, Reserve Affairs & Logistics)

(947369)

CPSIA information can be obtained
at www.ICGtesting.com
Printed in the USA
BVHW081123200820
586901BV00014B/2538

F-16 Integrated Logistics Support: Still Time To Consider Economical Alternatives: LCD-80-89

U.S. Government Accountability Office (GAO)

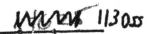

BY THE COMPTROLLER GENERAL

Report To The Congress

OF THE UNITED STATES

F-16 Integrated Logistics Support: Still Time To Consider Economical Alternatives

While the Air Force's integrated logistics support plan for the F-16 should ensure that the aircraft will be adequately maintained, there is still time and opportunity to improve its effectiveness and reduce support costs.

This report recommends several alternative operational and support concepts which Department of Defense and Air Force logistics planners need to consider for the still developing F-16 program.

113055

011723

LCD-80-89

AUGUST 20, 1980